The Kids' Career Library™

A Day in the Life of a
Veterinarian

Mary Bowman-Kruhm

The Rosen Publishing Group's

PowerKids Press™
New York

Thanks to Dr. Marcia Vandermause and the Frederick, MD, Mobile Veterinary Clinic.

Published in 1999 by The Rosen Publishing Group, Inc.
29 East 21st Street, New York, NY 10010

First Edition

Book Design: Erin McKenna

Photo Illustrations: All photo illustrations by Ethan Zindler.

Bowman-Kruhm, Mary.
    A day in the life of a veterinarian / by Mary Bowman-Kruhm.
        p.   cm. — (The kids' career library)
    Includes index.
    Summary: Follows a veterinarian as she makes house calls to take care of a variety of animals.
    ISBN 0-8239-5296-7
    1. Veterinarians—Juvenile literature. 2. Veterinary medicine—Vocational guidance—Juvenile literature.
    3. Vandermause, Marcia—Juvenile literature. [1. Veterinarians. 2. Occupations.]
    I. Title. II. Series.
SF756.B68 1998
636.089'023—dc21
                                                                                98-15980
                                                                                CIP
                                                                                AC

Manufactured in the United States of America

Contents

An Early Start

Dr. Marcia Vandermause is a **veterinarian** (VET-er-ih-NAYR-ee-un). Unlike most vets, Dr. Marcia makes house calls! She takes care of small animals in their homes. Each morning at 8:00, Dr. Marcia checks her answering machine. She calls all of the people who left messages and sets up times when she will visit their pets. Then Dr. Marcia climbs into the van. This is her office on wheels.

"First, we have to help Bruiser," she tells Scotty, her helper. "It's an **emergency** (ee-MER-jen-see)."

◀ Dr. Marcia and Scotty keep their supplies for the day in their van.

Stuck!

Bruiser is a big white dog. He has his huge head stuck between two railings of the stairs.

"Easy, boy," says Dr. Marcia gently. Bruiser likes Dr. Marcia and he isn't afraid. He just wants his head free! Scotty and Dr. Marcia work carefully.

At last, Bruiser is free. Dr. Marcia checks his neck and head to make sure he isn't hurt. Her **pager** (PAY-jer) beeps while she's checking Bruiser. Someone is calling Dr. Marcia. "May I use your phone?" Dr. Marcia asks Bruiser's owner.

Dr. Marcia gives each animal the attention it deserves. ▶

Farm Animals

Pets aren't the only animals who see a veterinarian when they're sick or in need of a check-up. Animals that live on farms, such as horses and pigs, sometimes need a doctor's care too.

A veterinarian may visit a farm to take care of a cow that isn't giving milk or a horse that is **lame** (LAYM). The vet may even help out if an animal on the farm is giving birth. This vet has had special training in taking care of larger animals.

Farm animals usually don't need a vet's care as often as pets do. But special vets are there in case a farm animal needs help.

9

Another Emergency

Dr. Marcia and Scotty drive quickly to the house where Star lives.

"Star has been sick all morning," her owner says.

Dr. Marcia **examines** (eg-ZAM-inz) the dog. Then she sees a trash can that is turned over.

"I think Star got into the garbage," Dr. Marcia tells Star's owner. "Here's some **medicine** (MED-ih-sin) for her stomach. She should be fine in a day or two. And keep the lid tight on the trash can."

Dr. Marcia will work hard to find out what might be wrong with an animal. Even if it's right under her nose! ▶

The Cat in the Bathroom

On her next visit, Dr. Marcia knows she will find Lady Jane Grey Cat in the bathroom. Jane doesn't like to be examined and Dr. Marcia doesn't like to chase her. So Jane's owners put her in the bathroom to wait.

Jane sneezes. Her eyes are watery. She has a cold. As soon as Dr. Marcia is finished checking her, Jane races from the bathroom.

"Give her these pills twice a day until they are all gone. They will make her feel better," says Dr. Marcia to Jane's owners.

◄ Dr. Marcia is extra careful with animals that are very scared.

Tooth Trouble

The next visit is to see a very large dog called a **mastiff** (MAS-tif).

"I think Buster has a tooth that's hurting him," says his owner. "He paws at his mouth and **whimpers** (WIM-perz)."

Scotty soothes Buster while Dr. Marcia checks Buster's teeth.

"His teeth need to be cleaned. And one needs to be pulled. May I come back Monday morning?"

As they drive away, Dr. Marcia tells Scotty, "Buster is big but gentle. Our next patient is tiny but terrible!"

Animals don't have dentists to check their teeth. Instead, they rely on vets like Dr. Marcia. ▶

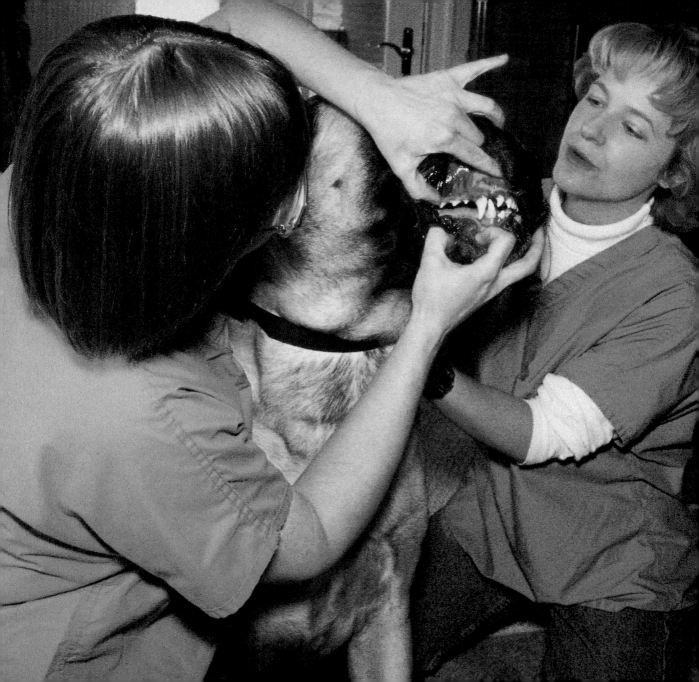

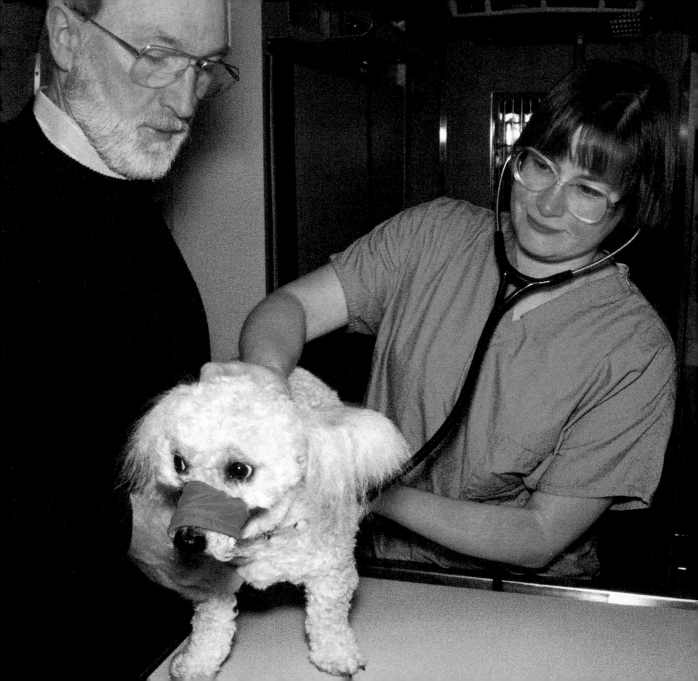

Terry the Terrible

Time for Terry's check-up! Like people, animals should be examined every year by their doctor to make sure they are healthy.

"Grrrrr," growls Terry.

Dr. Marcia knows not to touch even a small, cute dog that is growling. She gives Terry's owner a **muzzle** (MUZ-uhl) to put over Terry's nose. The muzzle doesn't hurt and keeps Terry from snapping or biting.

"You're fine," Dr. Marcia says to Terry after the check-up. Dr. Marcia takes off the muzzle. Terry runs happily into the yard.

◀ A pet's health is important. But Dr. Marcia's safety when she examines him is also important.

Franklin the Friendly Ferret

In town, Dr. Marcia stops at a house where a **ferret** (FEH-ret) named Franklin lives. Franklin is taking a ride on his owner's shoulder when Dr. Marcia gets there.

Dr. Marcia gives Franklin a shot for **rabies** (RAY-beez). The shot protects ferrets from this **disease** (dih-ZEEZ). This is the same disease as the one that dogs and cats get.

As Dr. Marcia and Scotty leave, Franklin crawls into his favorite box. He loves to play in it.

All pets should get their shots to stay healthy—even ferrets! ▶

Last Visit of the Day

A puppy greets Dr. Marcia with a friendly tail wag. He smells her and wiggles as she examines him. Then she gives him the shots he needs to stay well.

The young boy who owns the puppy watches. "We got him at the **animal shelter** (AN-ih-mul SHEL-ter)," he says.

"You picked a fine, healthy puppy. And adopting a pet from the shelter gives a good home to an animal that needs one," Dr. Marcia says.

◄ Being a good pet owner means taking care of his health too.

A Pet Is for Life

The last stop of the day is at the gas station. The van must be ready for Dr. Marcia to visit more pets tomorrow.

"A pet is just like a member of the family. Every pet deserves care and love," Dr. Marcia tells Scotty.

"I love my job," she adds. "I like to keep animals well, and help them get better if they're sick or hurt."

Glossary

animal shelter (AN-ih-mul SHEL-ter) A place to keep animals until homes are found for them.

disease (dih-ZEEZ) Illness that makes us sick.

emergency (ee-MER-jen-see) A sudden need for quick action.

examine (eg-ZAM-in) To look at something closely and carefully.

ferret (FEH-ret) A small animal that is related to weasels, skunks, and otters.

lame (LAYM) Having a hurt leg or foot.

mastiff (MAS-tif) A very large breed of dog.

medicine (MED-ih-sin) A drug a doctor gives to treat an illness.

muzzle (MUZ-uhl) A cloth or strap that is put around the mouth and keeps it closed.

pager (PAY-jer) A small machine that fits into a pocket and is used for receiving calls from other people.

rabies (RAY-beez) A disease animals can get and give to humans if the animal bites them.

veterinarian (VET-er-ih-NAYR-ee-un) A doctor who treats animals.

whimper (WIM-per) A small crying sound.

Index